Plain
An Apology

Cho

ISBN: 978-1-913642-57-0

Book designed by Aaron Kent

Edited by Aaron Kent

Broken Sleep Books (2021), Talgarreg, Wales

Contents

Plain Air:
An Apology in Transit

Cat Chong

Introduction

I return to The Long Walk (Windsor, United Kingdom) to read Cat Chong's debut. This spot is on a major Heathrow flight path. I count the time between each overhead plane – Virgin Atlantic, British Airways, something blue and undecipherable – 1 minute 34 seconds. The cries of a red kite are heard over the low murmurs of each engine. Chong might describe my location as a 'palimpsestic oversite'; a space that remains 'in the back and forth'.

Mirroring my immediate surroundings, the site of Chong's durational poem remains in a state of transit. The reader moves between the London Underground, a poppyseed bagel, a binder, pharmaceutical packaging, and a vending-machine coffee cup. Chong meditates on what it means to occupy a body that resides in the in-between – between location, between gender, between diagnosis, between career stage. The poetic voice momentarily inhabits shapes, songs, moments, and conversations – lingering at points, before moving onward. The body in transit is met with shifts in language. The *Duolingo* app expands the vocabulary, whilst 'crip' is reclaimed for the poet's 'word dictionary'. The sentence is no longer contained by punctuation.

Yet the work is littered with containers which are permanent and unwavering, offering a violent contrast to the flickering language of the poem. Codeine tablets pop-forth from blister packaging whilst prebiotic sachets haunt the page. An association between 'pain and plastic' is accumulated, as the reader comes to realise the 'carbon cost' of a body in transit.

Plain Air: An Apology in Transit is a remarkable and necessary debut.

(Briony Hughes)

Plain Air: An Apology in Transit takes the reader on a journey of uneasy motion, environmental guilt, and aching moments of stillness. It exists, in of itself, in a state of transition. The first iteration of the work sits in boxes alongside other medical ephemera and loose leaf poetry, part of a collaborative project between Chong and I for the 2019 Small Press Book fair. Hand cut and stapled, each page sliced into twelve wispy strips, moving independently of each other. The second iteration was a live reading in the Poetry Cafe basement. The visuals projected onto Chong while they read in the darkened room. The last time I saw them in person before their own transition to living in Singapore (this is denoted by my sniffles heard in the footage). And now, the third iteration is this pamphlet. Text jostles without pause on each page, like commuters on a packed early morning train or a disabled body feeling the relentlessness of movement. *Plain Air* is a poignant and demonstration of the relationship between poetry and bodies in motion. The poet's own meditations and deliberations are thoughtfully measured against every date, train time, and milligram.

(E. P. Jenkins)

It is October seventh 2019 and extinction rebellion are
rebelling I take a train into London from my home
into London I walk to the station that is 9 minutes
away from my house nine minutes of movement
My body still has a carbon cost of something I take
the train into London to see my friends I take the
underground between Waterloo and Euston I feel
compelled to walk To walk between the University of
London institutions for the first time since crossing
between 'student' and 'unemployed' UCL Birkbeck
SOAS I see my friends and we talk about poetry I take
the underground between Tottenham Court Road
and Waterloo I take the train back When I arrive at my
station Ray my dad has driven to meet me He insists
on driving to meet me because it is dark because I am
alone because I occupy the shape of a woman because
I am disabled and he knows that I am tired insists on

driving me home despite the fact that it is close to midnight he drives me home I eat dinner at half 12 I eat the leftovers I left for myself later When I have the energy to cook to eat I am able to be vegan I take a hot drink to bed containing Bimuno powder to counter the long term side effects of prolonged opioid use Each small pouch of powder sealed in unrecyclable plastic Snip it open There's always a small collection of tablets at my bedside I am disabled and an improved quality of life is pushed popped out of plastic packaging each evening each morning 30 milligrams at a time Plastic that also isn't recyclable [WHAT IS CODEINE MADE OF?] I am half reluctant to know what refined substances I have committed to in a state of reliance Named after the Ancient Greek κώδεια meaning 'poppy head' I have a poppy head I am a poppy head I have a head full of poppies The flowers placed in wreath pinned on shirts in remembrance The seeds which devastated South East Asia in the 1850s displaced millions of Chinese the First Opium War of 1839 – 1842 the Second Opium War of 1856 – 1860 encouraged in Singapore by the British colonial government as it reaped profit from opium licenses I'm unable to distance myself from being intimately bound up with these violences *Codeine can be extracted directly from the plant, most codeine is synthesized from the much more abundant morphine found in opium poppies* Last month the manufacturer changed from Teva UK Limited to Crescent Pharma Ltd From the*leading provider of medicines to the NHS* To one that *covers therapeutic areas* including antibiotics anticoagulants and painkillers The next day I add 'crip' to my Word dictionary I go back into London on October 15th extinction rebellion have been banned from rebelling in London I am an hour early I sit in a Pret near the river "Do you want it, it's free?" I don't know his name he offers Lovingly Handmade Pret Bar Full Of Fruit Goodness *This bar is full of goodness* It goes off today I accept the moralism in flapjack form No time or energy to eat before the seminar I am complicit within the single use plastic economy as I refuse food waste I am alone accompanied by Oh Wonder's single Hallelujah *I heard it on the radio on my way back home* I lip sync each word and evoke praise and thanks for my continued being Inquiring to who Each act of divine Briony There I made the reference it made me happy too I am communal I will have to fly by plane just before the new year I start helping out in my parent's garden They grow tomatoes carrots aubergines edamame garlic courgettes squashes apples figs I will never be able to carbon offset the footprint I will make have made I look into accommodation at the university I won't have a kitchen When I cook here I get to be vegan That won't be possible anymore To write about travel as a form of ecological movement across recycled material I travel into London and sit in a room of medics and think about contested interdisciplinary boundaries They talk about medical humanities as humanities belonging to medicine I long for I look for contemporary experimental poetics in every room I enter to retain an elusive formation of identity I will change I know I hope I will be kind A few weeks later I will hear someone say "We separate the disciplines so that we can be interdisciplinary" Perhaps writing in the space over British Rail lines is a form of palimpsestic oversite writing a mind the gap over sight response writing I am notified about my first academic interview 23 hours before it's due to take place In the days subsequent I am encapsulated within the tenderhooks of waiting Tenterhooks as a mishearing Duolingo tells me that one day one apple and the doctor won't be looking for me I get sick with sleeplessness and worry I take 1000mg ofvitamin C Other supplements induce retching and nausea This is not the first time this has happened I travel into London again and again I am tired of waiting to see if I am wanted It is October 28th Oh Wonder release an acoustic iteration of Better Now an addition of new lyrics *I can't help dreaming of the day When you're not laying in a room of strangers Morphine dancing in your veins You will be okay* All air evacuates the song for a moment at 53 seconds again at 59 Images of waiting hours Hot vending machine cups of coffee gone cold Beeps which align with the train Doors opening on my way back and forth between home into the capital I think I may never learn to drive On November 17th I take the train to his home for the last time Officially 'partner' designated for his national security clearance I question the possibility of romance mediated by an act of government surveillance I buy a poppy seed bagel as an act of autonomy to confidently fail a drug test I am in transit and intransigent It is November 4th I take the train and the underground EP Jenkins gifts me with a cloth wrapped parcel of lavender bergamot camomile salt and ash "Top secret witch ☺ remedy" It is the first plastic free anti-inflammatory I've received in over 2 years The last was morphine sulphate in a glass bottle A partial subversion of the intimate association between pain and plastic My binder is 78% Polyamide 22% Elastane Outer 67% Nylon 33% Lycra Microfibre Inner Back 100% Cotton Inner

Front I take the train home Arriving at 22:53 I take my makeup off Put my pyjamas on Make myself a hot drink of oat milk Horlicks dissolving one sachet of Bimuno powder I go to bed and push out 30mg of Codeine

References

@Teva_UK,2012. *Twitter:TevaUK.* [Online] Available at: https://twitter.com/teva_uk?lang=en [Accessed 1 November 2019].

Crescent Pharma Ltd., 2011. *The Pharmacist: Crescent Pharma Ltd.* [Online] Available at: https://www.thepharmacist.co.uk/c40-company-profiles-a-z/c42-company-profiles-a-z/crescent-pharma-ltd/
[Accessed 31 October 2019].

Gillott, B., 2019. *Reading John Cage, With and Without Tone.* London, Contemporary Innovative Poetry Research Seminar.

University of Calgary, 2010. *Unlocking the opium poppy's biggest secret: Genes that make codeine, morphine.* [Online] Available at: https://www.sciencedaily.com/releases/2010/03/100314150916.htm
[Accessed 1 November 2019].

Vander Gucht, J. & West, A., 2019. *Better Now (Acoustic).* [Sound Recording] (Oh Wonder).

Vander Gucht, J. & West, A., 2019. *Hallelujah.* [Sound Recording] (Oh Wonder).

Acknowledgements

Thank you E.P. Jenkins, all this started with you, in chronic fusion and crip solidarity. You have my heart – my disabled joy begins with you.

Thank you Briony Hughes, Laura Hellon, Honey and Bumble Hellon-Hughes for holding me through the hardest of times, despite being so far away you've never left my side.

Thank you to my family, both biological and found, for the depth and sincerity of your love. Thank you Ray, Carol, Jane, and Richard for giving me places to call home.

To all the lecturers at Royal Holloway University who have supported me, you have my deepest thanks; it means everything to look up to you. Thank you Redell Olsen, Robert Hampson, Prudence Bussey-Chamberlain, and Nisha Ramayya. Thank you Amy Evans Bauer too for your gifts of protections and care, thank you for holding space for me even in the most academic of spaces. I hold your generosity, compassion, and grace in every admiration, thank you for showing me the kindest ways for poets to be in the world. I couldn't wish for better mentors.

I would like to express my gratitude to the Poetics Research Centre who first gave this work a place at the table as part of the Small Publishers Fair 2019. Thank you to everyone who sat with me in the Green Room to hear this poem in its first reading.

Thank you to the poetics doctoral candidates including Caroline Harris, Sarah Cave, Astra Papachristodoulou, Karen Sandhu, Nadira Wallace, and Sarah Dawson. Your care and commitment to community has taught me everything I know.

To JD Howse and 'Permeable Barrier', I am indebted to you, thank you for the time and consideration with which you've approached all my work. Thank you for seeing this poem through so many iterations and for helping it every step of the way.

Aaron Kent, thank you for being the most wonderful editor, thank you for believing in this unrest.

And finally, to my partner Stephen Mallet, thank you for every shelter, safety, and act of care.

LAY OUT YOUR UNREST

Lightning Source UK Ltd.
Milton Keynes UK
UKHW050708200521
384043UK00006B/38

9 781913 642570